Original title:
Dreams Under the Stars

Copyright © 2024 Creative Arts Management OÜ
All rights reserved.

Author: Alec Davenport
ISBN HARDBACK: 978-9916-90-614-9
ISBN PAPERBACK: 978-9916-90-615-6

The Cosmic Cradle

In the arms of the stars we sway,
Whispers of dreams in the Milky Way.
Cradled in stardust, soft and bright,
Guided by the moon's gentle light.

Galaxies twirl in a dance divine,
Universes breathe, their secrets entwined.
Cradled by night, we find our place,
Lost in the vastness, a warm embrace.

Elysium of the Night

Silvery shadows cast by the moon,
In the garden of dreams, wildflowers bloom.
A symphony of stars in a velvet sky,
Whispered secrets as nightbirds fly.

In the calm embrace of twilight's glow,
The heart beats softly, gentle and slow.
A world awakened in hues of blue,
In Elysium, love feels anew.

Universe Between Heartbeats

Between each breath, galaxies flow,
Waves of time in a ceaseless flow.
Moments stretch like infinite space,
In the silence, we find our grace.

With every heartbeat, worlds collide,
Echoes of dreams that love can't hide.
A universe vast, yet close at hand,
In the rhythm of life, we understand.

Celestial Boughs of Hope

Under the canopy of stars, we roam,
Finding our peace, our sweet, safe home.
Branches of light, they cradle our fate,
Whispers of hope in the night create.

With every dawn, the promise renews,
Painting the skies in vibrant hues.
Celestial boughs, reaching so high,
In the arms of the cosmos, we learn to fly.

The Astral Compass

In the night sky, stars are bright,
Guiding souls with gentle light.
Each constellation tells a tale,
Of journeys taken through the veil.

With every twinkle, dreams take flight,
Navigating through the silent night.
The compass points to worlds unseen,
Where hopes and wishes dance between.

A Tapestry of Night Whispers

Threads of darkness softly weave,
In moonlit hours, we believe.
Whispers linger in the air,
Secrets held with tender care.

Each breeze carries gentle sighs,
As shadows play beneath the skies.
A tapestry of dreams unfolds,
In stories shared, the night enfolds.

Starlight's Golden Promise

Beneath the stars, a promise glows,
In every shimmer, love bestows.
Golden beams of hope arise,
Lighting paths where courage lies.

As twilight wraps the earth in grace,
We find our peace in starlit space.
A dance of fate, hand in hand,
Together we shall make our stand.

The Milky Way's Embrace

Under a quilt of endless night,
The Milky Way glimmers, pure delight.
Stars like whispers dance and play,
In the cosmic arms, we dream away.

Waves of starlight softly sweep,
Awakening secrets the heavens keep.
Where time stands still, we float as one,
In the vast embrace, our hearts are spun.

A Symphony of Stars

In the stillness of nighttime air,
Notes of brilliance, beyond compare.
Each star sings a tale of old,
In the concert of wonders, bright and bold.

The universe plays its timeless tune,
Under the watch of a silver moon.
Harmonies weave through darkened skies,
As we lose ourselves in starry sighs.

Night's Enchanted Pathways

Through a tapestry of shimmering light,
We wander beneath the velvet night.
Paths of stardust lead us near,
To the secrets only dreamers hear.

Moonbeams guide our gentle steps,
In a world where time intercepts.
With every heartbeat, magic grows,
In these enchanted woods, we chose.

Gleaming Stars on Silent Waters

Silent waters mirror the sky,
Reflecting dreams as we pass by.
Gleaming stars paint the surface bright,
As we drift softly into the night.

Rippling whispers caress the shore,
With each glance, we long for more.
In this calm embrace, we find our peace,
Where time and tides whisper sweet release.

The Cosmos of Sleep

In twilight's embrace, dreams softly weave,
Stars whisper secrets that night shall conceive.
Floating on clouds, we drift through the dark,
Awakening visions, igniting the spark.

Shadows of stillness, where silence cascades,
Time bends and curtails, as slumber invades.
The cosmos unfolds, in layers it flows,
Cradling our minds where wonder bestows.

A Starlit Tapestry

Upon the heavens, threads of gold gleam,
Each star a story, each light a dream.
Woven together in nocturnal art,
Binding the night with a shimmering heart.

Constellations whisper, in gentle tones,
Mapping our fates in celestial stones.
A tapestry bright, with colors that sing,
Under the gaze of the moon's silver ring.

The Night's Secret Chamber

In shadows concealed, the chamber lies still,
Old echoes of wisdom, the air gently fills.
Whispers of ages, with stories to tell,
Adventures await in this enchanting shell.

Heartbeats resound, like footsteps in gloom,
The night wraps around, like a shroud in a room.
Hidden in corners, mysteries roam,
Inviting the curious to seek out a home.

Radiance of the Unknown

In darkness it glows, a light yet unseen,
Flickering softly, like hope in between.
The dance of the shadows, a delicate play,
Illuminating paths that lead us away.

With every heartbeat, a spark draws us near,
To realms uncharted, where dreams disappear.
A radiance whispers, promising grace,
In the arms of the unknown, we find our place.

Echoes of the Moonlit Path

Whispers dance beneath the trees,
Silver beams in gentle breeze,
Footsteps soft on forest ground,
Nature's secrets all around.

Shadows play with dreams alight,
Guiding stars through velvet night,
Each soft sigh, a tale unfolds,
In the dark, a treasure holds.

Crickets sing a lullaby,
While the nightingale takes flight,
Echoes of the moonlit path,
Lead us gently, steer our math.

In silent woods, the spirits glow,
With every turn, new wonders show,
Step by step, through twilight's grace,
We'll find our heart's most sacred place.

Constellation's Lullaby

Twinkling lights up in the sky,
Stars that whisper, wink, and sigh,
Galaxies in grand parade,
Softest dreams in starlight laid.

Comets trace a fleeting path,
In their wake, a cosmic bath,
Each star a wish, each wish a song,
Guiding us where we belong.

The Milky Way, a shimmering stream,
Fills our hearts with hope and dream,
Celestial choirs hum and chime,
A lullaby for weary time.

As we gaze upon the night,
We find solace, pure delight,
In the vastness, we unite,
Underneath the stars so bright.

Wandering Through the Milky Haze

In the twilight, softly glows,
Whispers of the cosmos flows,
Each step taken, a journey vast,
Through the milky haze, we cast.

Nebulas in colors swirl,
In this magic, dreams unfurl,
With each breath, the universe,
Fills our hearts, we silently traverse.

Galactic tides pull us near,
As we drift without a fear,
Stars above hold tales untold,
In their light, our souls unfold.

On this path of endless night,
We embrace the cosmic flight,
Wandering through, lost yet found,
In the beauty all around.

Ethereal Journeys

Floating softly on the breeze,
Hearts awakened, at such ease,
In the dawn of whispered dreams,
Life unfolds with gentle seams.

In the garden of the night,
Hidden wonders steeped in light,
Every petal holds a truth,
Crafted carefully, eternal youth.

Through the mist, we rise and soar,
Seeking tales of yesteryear,
On the wings of hope we fly,
Chasing stars across the sky.

In these journeys, we embrace,
All the beauty time can grace,
Ethereal whispers call us near,
As we navigate without fear.

The Universe's Tender Song

In whispers soft, the stars conspire,
They sing of dreams, they spark a fire.
A symphony in cosmic dance,
Where every heart can find its chance.

The moonlit glow, a gentle guide,
With every pulse, the worlds collide.
In vast horizons, secrets lie,
A melody that fills the sky.

Fragments of a Starlit Dream

Scattered light on velvet seas,
Each twinkling star, a whispered breeze.
A tapestry of hope we weave,
In night's embrace, we dare believe.

In depths of dark, our spirits soar,
Beyond the veil, we seek for more.
With every breath, the silence gleams,
In fragments found, we chase our dreams.

Infinity Awaits

Among the stars, a pathway gleams,
Where time dissolves and wisdom beams.
In every pulse of cosmic light,
Infinity calls through endless night.

The galaxies spin, a dance so rare,
Whispering secrets into the air.
In the quiet vastness of this space,
We find our truth, we find our place.

Beneath the Veil of Night

Beneath the cloak of velvet sky,
The universe breathes a gentle sigh.
Stars like lanterns, guiding souls,
In the dark, our spirit rolls.

Soft shadows play in the moon's embrace,
Each heartbeat echoes, a timeless trace.
In the stillness, we hear the call,
Beneath the night, we are one and all.

Embrace of the Night Sky

Underneath the velvet dome,
Stars whisper secrets of the roam.
Moonlight bathes the world in peace,
Time itself seems to release.

The breeze carries tales untold,
In the dark, the heart feels bold.
Constellations dance and play,
Guiding dreams that drift away.

Each twinkle breeds a silent wish,
Captured in the midnight's swish.
Crickets sing their lullabies,
Harmonizing with our sighs.

In the stillness, shadows sway,
Embracing night, come what may.
With each breath, the cosmos sighs,
A tapestry of endless skies.

Celestial Reflections

Mirrored in the quiet lake,
Stars above begin to wake.
Ripples form, a soft embrace,
Nature holds a sacred space.

Galaxies in shimmering dance,
Inviting us to take a chance.
The universe, a beckoning call,
To each seeker, great or small.

Planets glide, a graceful flight,
Through the vastness of the night.
Every glance, a story spun,
In the cosmos, we are one.

With every breath, the silence sings,
Echoing the joy that living brings.
In the depths, reflections say,
Life is magic in its way.

Myriad Silhouettes of the Cosmos

Shapes emerge in starlit haze,
Whispering tales of ancient days.
nebulae stretch in colors bright,
As shadows play in cosmic light.

Figures dance in stellar grace,
Each a dream, a lost embrace.
Glimmers spark in the endless flow,
Painting patterns in dark's glow.

Constellations weave their art,
Mapping journeys of the heart.
Celestial bodies take their stand,
Guardians of this wondrous land.

In their silhouettes, we find,
Connections forged in heart and mind.
With each gaze into the deep,
The universe calls us to leap.

Shadows in the Astral Light

Beneath the stars, shadows blend,
In the night, where stories tend.
Luminescence plays its tune,
Guiding hearts beneath the moon.

Lost in the ether, time stands still,
Every moment a quiet thrill.
A dance of light with shadows cast,
Memories tethered to the past.

Galactic whispers fill the air,
Inviting us to dream and dare.
In the stillness, secrets flow,
Revealing truths we yearn to know.

In the astral light, we find
A piece of comfort for the mind.
As shadows weave through starry nights,
Hope ignites in the softest lights.

Sojourns in the Celestial Sea

Sailing upon the starlit tide,
Whispers of dreams, where shadows reside.
Galaxies dance in the velvet dark,
Echoes of laughter leave their mark.

Waves of light in a cosmic play,
Guiding lost souls to the break of day.
With each twinkling star, a path unfolds,
Adventures written in stories untold.

Beneath the moon's benevolent gaze,
Time slows down in this endless maze.
We drift through realms beyond our ken,
In the celestial sea, we are children again.

With hearts alight and spirits free,
We wander through eternity.
Each moment a treasure, bold and bright,
Sojourns in the celestial night.

Beneath the Infinite Canopy

Underneath the canopy so vast,
Whispers of nature, a spell is cast.
Leaves that flutter, stars that gleam,
Life unfolds like a wondrous dream.

Crickets serenade in the twilight hush,
Night blooms forth in a tranquil rush.
Fireflies dance, with their gentle light,
The world awakens in the soft night.

Each breath a promise, each glance a chance,
To lose oneself in this ancient dance.
Beneath the sky's eternal embrace,
We find our rhythm, we find our place.

Moments twinkle like gems on a thread,
Stories untold in the silence bred.
We walk as one, no longer alone,
In the infinite canopy, we've found our home.

The Night's Whimsy

Draped in shadows, the night comes alive,
With secrets tucked where the moonbeams thrive.
A gentle breeze spins tales in the dark,
Every flicker upon the sky's arc.

Laughter spills from the stars above,
Weaving dreams with threads of love.
The night sings sweet in its gentle tone,
A world unveiled, no longer lone.

Cupcakes frosted with the milky way,
Comets racing, come out and play.
In the stillness, where wishes abide,
Magic shimmers on the moonlit ride.

With each heartbeat, the night reveals,
A treasure trove of hearts that heals.
In the night's whimsy, we'll take our flight,
Two souls, entwined, in the velvet night.

Cosmic Whispers

In the quiet, when stars ignite,
Cosmic whispers fill the night.
Thoughts drift softly like cosmic dust,
In the universe, we place our trust.

Messages swirl in the astral sea,
Tales of wonder, wild and free.
Each twinkle, a story from the past,
In every heartbeat, the die is cast.

Galaxies bend in a dance divine,
Echoing secrets, yours and mine.
Through trials and triumphs, we boldly roam,
Finding our way in the vast unknown.

Listening close, the heart will hear,
Cosmic whispers, crystal clear.
Together we journey, your hand in mine,
Bound by the stars, forever entwined.

A Starlit Journey to Nowhere

Underneath the endless sky,
Whispers of the night pass by.
Stars like lanterns, softly glow,
Guiding dreams where no one knows.

Clouds drift softly, shadows play,
Time stands still, then slips away.
Paths unwritten call my name,
In this journey, nothing's the same.

Footsteps echo on the ground,
Lost in thoughts, no way is found.
Each twinkle hints at tales untold,
In the dark, the heart grows bold.

The Night's Tender Embrace

Moonlight spills like silver rain,
Kissing softly, easing pain.
In its glow, my fears take flight,
Wrapped in shadows, lost in night.

Whispers glide on evening's breath,
Each one cradles life and death.
Stars above like watchful eyes,
Guard my dreams as silence sighs.

A blanket woven of the dark,
Every heartbeat leaves a mark.
In this stillness, love is found,
In the night, we're safe and sound.

Sails of Dreams on Cosmic Waters

Charting courses through the void,
Sails unfurled, the heart's employed.
Stars my compass, waves my guide,
In this vastness, none can hide.

Every shimmer, every spark,
Carries whispers through the dark.
With each breath, I drift away,
Floating on the night's ballet.

Galaxies in silent flight,
Paint the canvas of the night.
Time is but a fleeting thought,
In this sea, I'm always caught.

Beyond the Horizon of Sleep

Dreams will carry us so far,
Past the realms of who we are.
In the stillness, worlds collide,
Hopes and fears no longer hide.

Softly wrapped in twilight's haze,
Through the shadows, we will gaze.
Every heartbeat sings a song,
Here in dreams, we both belong.

Beyond horizons, futures gleam,
In our hearts, there lies a dream.
With dawn's light, we'll rise anew,
Guided by the love we drew.

The Heart's Celestial Map

In the night sky's endless weave,
Stars align, a tale to believe,
Each twinkle holds a secret bold,
Stories of love, whispered and told.

With every pulse, the cosmos sighs,
Mapping dreams where freedom flies,
A heart's journey through boundless space,
In starlit dance, we find our place.

Sweet Surrender to the Night

As dusk descends with velvet grace,
The world slows down, finds its pace,
Moonlit whispers brush the ground,
In quiet peace, our souls are found.

Close your eyes, let shadows play,
In the stillness, fears decay,
Embrace the night, a gentle fight,
For in the dark, we find our light.

Stars' Embrace in Solitude

In solitude, the stars align,
A canvas vast, twinkling divine,
They cradle dreams upon their beams,
Whispering softly, echoing themes.

Alone we stand, yet never apart,
The universe lives within the heart,
Each shining orb, a guiding spark,
In celestial warmth, we find our mark.

Visions of a Celestial Heart

From cosmic depths, a vision starts,
Illuminating our hidden parts,
A heart ablaze with astral light,
It fuels our spirit through the night.

In vast horizons where hopes ignite,
We chase the dreams that feel so right,
With every beat, the heavens sing,
A dance of love, infinite spring.

Celestial Dances

Stars twinkle in the night,
Whispers of ancient light.
Galaxies spin and sway,
In the silence, dreams play.

Moonbeams cast a glow,
Softly where shadows flow.
Constellations weave their tale,
As the night winds gently sail.

Planets dance in harmony,
Waltzing through infinity.
Each twirl a cosmic song,
Echoing where we belong.

Gravity pulls us near,
To the universe, we cheer.
In this vast eternal sea,
We find our destiny.

Secrets in the Night

Beneath the cloak of dark,
Whispers flow like a spark.
Moonlit shadows start to creep,
Guarding secrets ours to keep.

Stars guard tales of the past,
In their glow, memories cast.
Echoes of lost dreams reside,
In the night where hopes abide.

Silence wraps the world in dreams,
As the starlight softly gleams.
Hidden truths, like constellations,
Awake our deep yearnings and aspirations.

With the dawn, those secrets fade,
Yet in our hearts, they are laid.
The night will always keep,
Dreams that softly, sweetly seep.

A Canvas of Cosmic Hues

Nebulas paint the sky,
With colors that mesmerize.
Splashes of pink and blue,
In the vastness, they renew.

Galaxies swirl in delight,
Crafting beauty in the night.
Every hue tells a tale,
Of worlds where visions sail.

Stars like brush strokes shine,
In the heavens, intertwine.
A canvas where dreams soar,
Inviting hearts to explore.

With each glance, we discern,
The wonders for which we yearn.
In this cosmic ballet,
Imagination finds its way.

Wandering Through Silver Light

Through the night, we wander free,
Guided by the starry sea.
Silver light leads our way,
In dreams, we gently sway.

Underneath the cosmic dome,
We find our place, our home.
Every beam a tender kiss,
Filling hearts with endless bliss.

Stardust whispers in the breeze,
Carrying our hopes with ease.
Weaving paths in moonlit glow,
Where the wildest thoughts can flow.

In this maze of light and dark,
We light our inner spark.
As we wander, hand in hand,
In this silver dreamland.

Dreams Woven in Twilight

In twilight's glow, the whispers rise,
Soft echoes dance beneath the skies.
Shadows weave a tapestry bright,
As dreams are spun in fading light.

Stars awaken, their secrets told,
Glittering tales of dreams so bold.
The night enfolds, a tender sigh,
Embracing wishes, set to fly.

Each heartbeat sings in muted tones,
As twilight wraps our weary bones.
In this hushed hour, hope takes flight,
A journey starts in soft twilight.

With every breath, the promise glows,
In silent realms where the wild wind blows.
Dreams woven deep, as night unfurls,
A magical world where peace twirls.

Celestial Hopes

Beneath a dome of starry light,
We gaze upon the endless night.
With every twinkle, hearts align,
In cosmic dance, our dreams entwine.

Hope sails high on comet trails,
Through cosmic winds where courage sails.
In galaxies where wishes bloom,
The universe dispels all gloom.

Celestial hopes like whispers play,
Guiding us through the darkest fray.
In astral seas, we chart our course,
With faith that rises, a mighty force.

In starry realms, our spirits soar,
As dreams ignite forevermore.
United by the glowing skies,
Celestial hopes forever rise.

Nightfall's Secret Garden

In shadowed glades where silence reigns,
A secret garden softly gains.
Petals whisper secrets old,
Of midnight tales yet to unfold.

Moonlight kisses every bloom,
As shadows scatter, dispelling gloom.
This hidden realm, a quiet grace,
Holds tender dreams in sweet embrace.

Where fireflies dance, our fears dissolve,
In nature's heart, we find resolve.
Each bloom reflects a whispered prayer,
In nightfall's garden, free and rare.

As stars peer down, a watchful crowd,
We weave our hopes, silently proud.
In this retreat away from strife,
Nightfall's garden breathes with life.

The Universe Beckons

The universe calls with a gentle voice,
Inviting us all to embrace our choices.
With swirling stars, we find our way,
To realms unknown where night meets day.

In every heartbeat, the cosmos sings,
Of distant worlds and unfathomed things.
Galaxies spin in a celestial dance,
Through the dark, we take our chance.

With eyes uplifted, we seek the light,
The universe beckons, bold and bright.
A journey woven with every hope,
In starlit dreams, we learn to cope.

As wonders bloom in endless sky,
We reach for more, we learn to fly.
In timeless space where dreams ignite,
The universe beckons, a guiding light.

A Night of Endless Possibilities

Stars twinkle softly in the dark,
Dreams awaken, igniting a spark.
The moonlight dances on the ground,
In silence, magic can be found.

Wishes float upon the breeze,
Carried softly through the trees.
With every glance at the night sky,
Hope unfolds as time slips by.

The world feels vast, yet close at hand,
Adventure waiting, just like planned.
Every heartbeat whispers a chance,
To embrace life in a daring dance.

So tread with courage, hearts aflame,
In this realm, we'll never be the same.
For a night of endless dreams awaits,
Along the path that love creates.

The Universe's Caress.

Glimmers fade into the night,
Galaxies spark with pure delight.
Cosmic whispers softly sway,
Guiding hearts that lose their way.

Stardust fills the air we breathe,
With every sigh, we dare believe.
Across the void, the echoes call,
Embracing all, both great and small.

The universe, a vast embrace,
Where dreams align in perfect space.
With every pulse, we feel it near,
A loving touch that conquers fear.

Wrapped in wonder, hand in hand,
In this moment, we will stand.
For the universe's sweet caress,
Awakens souls, brings happiness.

Whispers of Midnight Skies

In the hush of night so serene,
Stars reveal what might have been.
Softly, secrets ride the breeze,
Whispers carried through the trees.

Moonbeams cast a silver glow,
Illuminating dreams we sow.
In shadows deep, our hopes arise,
Bathed beneath the midnight skies.

Time suspends its fleeting flight,
As we dance in purest light.
With every breath, a chance to see,
The world unfold, just you and me.

Lost in wonder, hearts ablaze,
In this tapestry of gaze.
Each moment rich with endless sighs,
In the magic of midnight skies.

Celestial Reverie

Beneath the arch of twinkling stars,
We find the solace that is ours.
In realms of dreams and endless thoughts,
The universe, where hope is sought.

Galactic tales in silence spin,
Each heartbeat holds what lies within.
In swirling hues, our spirits soar,
To heights unseen, forevermore.

Among the constellations wide,
Our souls entwined, with none to hide.
A canvas painted with delight,
In sacred moments of the night.

So let us drift on this sweet breeze,
In celestial reverie, we seize.
For in this vast and wondrous play,
Our hearts will guide us on our way.

Starlit Fantasies

In the hush of night, dreams arise,
Whispers dance beneath the skies.
Light twinkles in the silent glow,
Where wishes float and hopes can grow.

Through fields of stars, we gently glide,
Heartbeats sync with the celestial tide.
Each shimmer tells a story bright,
Of magic spun in the velvet night.

Echoes of Twilight

As daylight fades, shadows creep,
The world sighs softly, starts to sleep.
Gentle hues of orange and blue,
Blend in the sky, a canvas anew.

Birds sing low, their songs rewind,
In twilight's arms, peace we find.
With every breath, the evening calls,
Echoes linger in twilight's halls.

Radiant Visions Above

High above, the dreams take flight,
With colors bright against the night.
Stars awaken, bold and clear,
They whisper secrets for those who hear.

Galaxies swirl in cosmic dance,
A symphony of chance and glance.
Each twinkling spark ignites the mind,
A radiant vision for us to find.

Moonlit Journeys

Under the moon's soft silver light,
We wander forth into the night.
Paths illuminated, shadows play,
Guiding our hearts along the way.

With every step, the world unfolds,
In quiet tales the night beholds.
Together we roam, spirits free,
On moonlit journeys, just you and me.

Stargazers' Ballet

Under the velvet sky we sway,
With twinkling lights leading the way.
Whispers of dreams in the night,
A dance of hope, pure and bright.

Moonlit steps on the grassy floor,
Each star a wish, we can't ignore.
Gravity lost in our embrace,
Together we float in this space.

We trace the paths of the light above,
Every glance whispers warmth and love.
In this vast universe so wide,
We find a home where we can hide.

As dawn approaches, shadows blend,
Our cosmic waltz begins to end.
Yet in our hearts, the light will stay,
Stargazers' ballet in endless play.

Ethereal Nocturnes

Soft lullabies weave through the dark,
Melodies played by the night's sweet spark.
Crickets sing with a tender cheer,
The moon listens close, crystal clear.

Breezes carry whispers of dreams,
Flowing gently like silver streams.
Each note drips from the sky's embrace,
Painting the night in a quiet grace.

Stars twinkle like the eyes of the wise,
They hold the secrets of endless skies.
In their glow, we find our way,
Guided by night till the break of day.

In chilling silence, our thoughts take flight,
Ethereal visions dance into sight.
As the world sleeps, we softly hum,
Nocturnes drift, and the magic comes.

Constellations of the Soul

In the canvas of night we seek,
Patterns stitched with a cosmic streak.
Every star, a story untold,
In constellations, our dreams unfold.

Galaxies whisper through the haze,
Echoes of love in a timeless phase.
We map our hearts in the starlit array,
Finding our paths in a magical way.

It's in the cosmic dance we find,
Reflections of the intertwined.
Each twinkle, a piece of our past,
Constellations that forever last.

Through the heavens, we wander free,
Chasing the light of destiny.
In the night sky, we find our goal,
A universe rich in the depths of soul.

Reveries in the Dark

In shadows deep, our thoughts take flight,
Whispering dreams in the still of night.
Each reverie, a spark of grace,
A secret world in this quiet space.

Stars flicker like the thoughts we keep,
In the heart's chamber, buried deep.
Drifting on whispers of twilight's breath,
Finding life in the dance of death.

Echoes of laughter lose their hold,
In memories painted in hues of gold.
Softly we tread on the edge of time,
In reveries lost, our spirits climb.

As night wraps us in its gentle cloak,
A symphony played with every stroke.
In this stillness, our dreams ignite,
Reveries shimmer in the quiet night.

Starlit Pathways

Beneath the sky so vast and bright,
We walk on trails of glittering light.
Each step we take, a dream unfolds,
With whispered tales that night beholds.

The air is crisp, the world at peace,
In starlit calm, our worries cease.
The universe sings a gentle tune,
As we dance beneath the watchful moon.

Guided by the stars, we drift and sway,
Lost in the magic of this array.
Every glimmer tells a tale of old,
Of cosmic journeys and secrets untold.

So let us wander, hand in hand,
On starlit pathways, a dreamland.
With every glance at the endless space,
Our hearts are filled with a quiet grace.

Moonbeam Memories

Softly glow the moon's embrace,
In its light, we find our place.
Moments captured, tender and true,
In silver beams that shine anew.

Each memory sparkles, bright and clear,
A dance of shadows, whispers near.
Time drifts slowly, like flowing streams,
We hold close our moonbeam dreams.

In twilight moments, stories weave,
A tapestry of what we believe.
With every sigh and every glance,
The moonlight leads us in a dance.

So let us treasure, night by night,
These moonbeam memories, pure delight.
For in their glow, we find our way,
Guided softly by the night's ballet.

Celestial Epiphanies

In the silence of the night, we find,
Celestial truths that bind the mind.
Stars align in a cosmic play,
Revealing secrets of the day.

In every twinkle, wisdom glows,
A quiet tide of thoughts that flows.
We glimpse the vastness of our fate,
In every moment, love awaits.

Let revelations spill like light,
Illuminating what feels right.
In the cosmos, we see the signs,
Guiding our hearts like ancient lines.

So take a breath, embrace the night,
In celestial epiphanies, take flight.
With every star, a spark, a chance,
To understand our cosmic dance.

Stardust Dreams

On a canvas of night, we softly gleam,
Bathed in the glow of stardust dreams.
With every wish tossed to the sky,
We unlock the wonders yet to fly.

In the space where hopes abide,
Where magic lingers, hearts collide.
Each twinkle carries a distant sigh,
A whisper of futures that may come by.

We weave our stories, bright and bold,
With threads of dreams that can't be sold.
In every heartbeat, a world anew,
A patchwork of visions, stitched in hue.

So let us chase what glimmers near,
In stardust dreams, we'll have no fear.
For in the night, our spirits soar,
Together we'll find what we're searching for.

Where Wishes Take Flight

In the whispering breeze, they soar,
Dreams take wing, forevermore.
Stars twinkle bright in the night,
Guiding hopes, pure and light.

Over mountains high, they dance,
Spinning tales of fate, romance.
Each wish, a feather, caught in the air,
Floating gently, released from despair.

With every heartbeat, stories unfold,
Twining secrets, daring and bold.
The horizon glows with a promise anew,
As wishes take flight to skies so blue.

Let them drift where the wild winds blow,
Into realms where only dreams know.
Lifted high, they awaken hearts,
In the realm where magic departs.

Skybound Fantasies

Clouds sail softly, dreams alight,
Chasing sunbeams, pure delight.
In the vastness, a canvas bright,
Colors weave in morning's light.

Whispers of wonders flirt with the air,
Painting visions, beyond compare.
Each thought a bird, freed from its cage,
Dancing through the sky, page by page.

Footprints in stars like dreams unfold,
Crafting secrets of the brave and bold.
In this realm where all hearts sigh,
Fantasies soar, reaching the sky.

Let imagination reach in flight,
Ending shadows, embracing light.
With each breath, we rise and sing,
In a world where our hopes take wing.

Nighttime's Resonant Stories

Under the blanket of twinkling stars,
Dreams whisper gently, near and far.
Moonlight glimmers on silent streams,
A tapestry woven from wishes and dreams.

Silver shadows rise and play,
With secrets of night, they softly sway.
Tales of love wrap the night,
In the embrace of soft twilight.

Each heartbeat resonates with the sky,
As echoes of stories learn to fly.
Through the hush, a lullaby calls,
Cradling the night as the daylight falls.

In the depths of the cosmos, whispers reside,
Celestial journeys we take in stride.
Nighttime's canvas, a magic unfurled,
Awakens the dreams in this wondrous world.

Echoes Beneath the Silver Sky

Beneath the silver canopy's glow,
Echoes of laughter begin to flow.
In the silent night, tales intertwine,
Painting memories softly, divine.

Stars hold stories from ages past,
Whispers of dreams that forever last.
With each pulse, the night breathes life,
Slicing through shadows, dispelling strife.

The moon sings softly, casting its spell,
Drowning the world in a shimmering well.
Every echo, a memory's trace,
Winding through time's intricate space.

As night unfolds, secrets ignite,
In the heart of the world, pure delight.
Under the silver sky's embrace,
All echoes unite, a sacred place.

When the World Goes Dark

When shadows creep and silence calls,
A hush descends, a stillness falls.
Stars blink out, one by one,
Night's embrace has just begun.

Whispers linger in the air,
Soft secrets cloaked in despair.
The heart beats slow, time stands still,
In darkness deep, we find our will.

Questions rise without a sound,
In this void, what can be found?
Hope flickers like a distant spark,
Illuminating paths from dark.

Yet even in the deepest night,
Courage stirs with hidden light.
When the world goes dark and cold,
Our stories yet remain untold.

Beneath the Lantern of the Moon

Underneath the moon's soft glow,
A tranquil sea begins to flow.
Waves of silver lap the shore,
A melody forevermore.

Whispers dance upon the breeze,
Carried secrets through the trees.
Shadows drift, they twist and turn,
Beneath the glow, our hearts will burn.

Stars above in quiet grace,
Illuminate this sacred space.
In the stillness, time suspends,
Where every moment softly bends.

Beneath the lantern's gentle light,
We find our hopes take flight tonight.
With every pulse, our spirits soar,
In harmony, we'll dream and explore.

Heartbeats in the Ether

In the silence, whispers dwell,
Heartbeats echo like a spell.
Transcending realms beyond the sight,
Connections forged in purest light.

Every pulse a story told,
Woven threads of warmth and cold.
In every thrum, we feel the grace,
A moment shared, a timeless place.

Voices travel on the wind,
Invisible threads tied and pinned.
Where two souls meet and then depart,
Leaving traces in the heart.

Through the ether, love will churn,
In every beat, a lesson learned.
Unified, we rise, we flow,
In sweet connection, we shall grow.

The Night's Allure

The night whispers with a soft embrace,
A velvet cloak, a secret place.
Mysteries wrapped in shadows deep,
Where dreams awake and memories sleep.

Stars unveil their twinkling eyes,
Guiding souls through midnight skies.
Lost in night's alluring charm,
We find solace, safe from harm.

Echoes linger, tales unfold,
Of love and courage, brave and bold.
Each precious moment, a wish cast wide,
In the night's allure, we safely bide.

Hold my hand as we drift along,
To the rhythm of the night's soft song.
Together we dance in time's embrace,
In the night's allure, we find our place.

Beneath the Cosmic Veil

Stars whisper secrets in the night,
Galaxies dance in shimmering light.
Dreams take flight on celestial winds,
Hopes awaken where the stardust spins.

Nebulas bloom in colors so rare,
Echoes of fate hang thick in the air.
Wanderers gaze with hearts laid bare,
Lost in the magic, they drift without care.

The cosmos hums a timeless song,
Where time and space together belong.
Infinite wonders, both near and far,
All come alive beneath each bright star.

Stardust Serenade

In the cradle of night, the world finds rest,
Singing soft melodies, the stars are blessed.
Whispers of dreams fill the velvet sky,
As echoes of laughter from ages gone by.

Light drapes the earth in a shimmering veil,
Each moment a treasure, a timeless tale.
Moonlight cascades like a silver stream,
In this stardust serenade, we all dream.

Celestial notes play a sweet refrain,
Binding our hearts in joy and in pain.
Lose yourself softly in space's embrace,
Find solace and wonder in this sacred place.

Nocturnal Visions

Shadows dance in the soft moonlight,
Creatures awaken, taking their flight.
The world is a canvas, painted in dreams,
Where nothing is ever as simple as seems.

With each breath, the night whispers low,
Stories of life in a cosmic flow.
Among the stars, visions unfold,
Revealing the magic, the mysteries untold.

Stars flicker gently, a cryptic code,
Guiding the way down this winding road.
Each moment a treasure, a fleeting sigh,
In the realm of nocturnal, our spirits fly.

The Night's Silken Embrace

Wrapped in shadows, the world grows still,
Time suspends as the night fulfills.
The moon drapes softly a silken shroud,
In this gentle quiet, we stand unbowed.

Stars twinkle brightly, a distant choir,
Filling the heart with a pulsing fire.
The night breathes life into dreams long sought,
Each wish carried on whispers of thought.

As the cool breeze plays through leaves so green,
We find ourselves lost in a world unseen.
Beneath the vast heavens, we find our place,
Cradled and cherished in the night's soft embrace.

The Twilight Chronicles

In the hush where shadows fade,
Whispers of twilight gently played.
Stars awaken, a soft embrace,
Time stands still, in this sacred space.

Beneath the veils of lavender night,
Dreams take wing, ready for flight.
Moonlight dances on the stream,
Fleeting moments, like a dream.

Colors blend in a muted hue,
A world reborn, fresh and new.
Stories linger in the air,
Echoes of love, hope, and care.

As the day surrenders its light,
The heart finds peace in the night.
With every breath, the twilight sighs,
Infinite wonders fill the skies.

Visions of Infinity

In the canvas of the boundless sky,
Galaxies swirl gently by.
A tapestry woven with cosmic thread,
Endless spirals where dreams are fed.

Stars converse in silent light,
Whispers that twist through the night.
Each twinkle a tale yet untold,
Fragments of wonders, brave and bold.

Time's river flows, an eternal stream,
Carrying echoes of every dream.
Through the corridors of space we soar,
Infinite visions that forever implore.

Boundless journeys await our sight,
In the glow of celestial light.
With every heartbeat, we reach for more,
In the vast expanse, we search and explore.

Threads of Silver Light

Woven softly through the trees,
Silver threads dance on the breeze.
Glimmers of fate in the evening glow,
Stories of the heart begin to flow.

In the twilight's gentle embrace,
Dreams emerge, a soft trace.
Whispers linger, sweet and low,
Guiding us where we wish to go.

Moments captured in glistening strands,
Ties that bind, like unseen hands.
A journey lit by love's pure spark,
Guiding us through the deepest dark.

With every shimmer, hope ignites,
In the tapestry of endless nights.
Threads of silver weave our fate,
Unity found in love's create.

The Nocturnal Odyssey

Through the shadows, we take flight,
In search of stories hidden from sight.
The moon our compass, stars our guide,
On a journey where dreams abide.

Whispers echo in the stillness deep,
Secrets of the night we seek to keep.
With every heartbeat, the world unfolds,
Mysteries wrapped in shadows bold.

Paths illuminated by ghostly gleams,
A symphony born from starlit dreams.
In this odyssey, we find our way,
Embraced by night, we dare to stay.

As dawn approaches, the stars recede,
But in our hearts, they'll always lead.
The night may fade, but its story thrives,
In the echoes of our daring lives.

Wandering Among the Celestial Lights

In the night sky, I tread so light,
Stars above me, twinkling bright.
Each step a dream, each breath a sigh,
Lost in wonder, I drift and fly.

Galaxies spin in the cosmic dance,
I reach for them, a fleeting chance.
Constellations guide me through the haze,
In their glow, I find my praise.

No boundaries set in this vast expanse,
I lose myself in the universe's trance.
Whispers of worlds far away call,
In their embrace, I feel so small.

With every heartbeat, the starlight weaves,
Stories told in the light of leaves.
Wandering where time meets the night,
Among the celestial, pure delight.

Beyond the Nebula

A veil of colors, a cosmic sea,
Luminous clouds beckon to me.
Diving deeper, where silence reigns,
Mysteries murmur in gentle strains.

Stars are born in this vibrant shroud,
A dance of life, both quiet and loud.
I drift through the haze, thoughts entwined,
Searching for truths the stardust defined.

Through shimmering gates, I make my path,
The universe whispers in quiet bath.
Each cosmic breath, a story retold,
Beyond the nebula, dreams unfold.

In the shadows where shadows fade,
Journeys began, and stardust laid.
Beyond the nebula, freedom's flight,
Chasing the dawn of eternal light.

Whispering Galaxies

Galaxies whisper in twilight skies,
Voices of old that softly rise.
Threads of light weave tales anew,
In cosmic realms, where stars pursue.

Each turning spiral, a dance so divine,
Radiates dreams that forever entwine.
Moonbeams guide the wayward heart,
Uniting worlds that drift apart.

Softly humming, the universe sings,
Cradling the hopes that starlight brings.
In the gentle fold of evening's grace,
The galaxies whisper, a warm embrace.

Through silence vast and darkened tides,
I listen close where wonder hides.
With every spark, a story ignites,
In the night air, whispering lights.

Celestial Whispers

In the dome of night, shadows wane,
Stars above, a celestial chain.
Whispers echo through the astral plane,
In their language, we share the same pain.

The moonlight dances on silver streams,
Carrying forth our secret dreams.
Galaxies shimmer in soft embrace,
Tracing the contours of time and space.

Each twinkling star, a tale to spin,
In each horizon, the journey begins.
Cosmic murmurs fill the void so wide,
In celestial whispers, we confide.

Fleeting moments of quiet bliss,
Woven tightly in the night's kiss.
Among the stars, our hearts entwine,
In celestial whispers, forever shine.

Astral Journeys

In the quiet night sky, we sail,
Through realms where dreams and starlight trail.
Winding paths in cosmic glows,
Whispers of secrets the universe knows.

Upon a comet's tail we ride,
Across the vastness, with stars as our guide.
Galaxies spin in a delicate dance,
Around us, the universe sings in a trance.

Time and space blend and twine,
In this astral dream, where all is divine.
Floating on currents of light and sound,
In the stillness of night, true peace is found.

As we journey through the celestial sea,
Every heartbeat a pulse of infinity.
Within the stars, our spirits ignite,
In the astral realm, we take flight.

Dancing with Celestial Bodies

Under shimmering skies, we glide,
With planets and moons, we joyfully bide.
In a waltz of light, we find our grace,
With each twirl, the universe we embrace.

Stars twinkle bright, our guiding spark,
In this ballet of night, igniting the dark.
Fluttering comets, like dancers on fire,
We join in the rhythm of our hearts' desire.

Galaxies swirl in a cosmic trance,
With every heartbeat, we take a chance.
The music of space calls out our names,
In this celestial dance, nothing remains the same.

As we spin through the ether, hand in hand,
Together we weave through astral strands.
In cosmic harmony, forever we'll roam,
In the arms of the heavens, we find our home.

Moonlit Fantasies

Beneath the silvered glow of the moon,
Dreams awaken, playing a gentle tune.
In whispers soft, the night unfolds,
Tales of wonder, in silence told.

Stars adorn the velvet sky,
As we drift on sighs, where spirits fly.
The moon our beacon, soft and bright,
Illuminating fantasies in the night.

Waves of silver kiss the land,
Guided by moonbeams, we take a stand.
In the hush of night, all fears recede,
Within our hearts, pure dreams we need.

With each breath, magic fills the air,
In moonlit realms, we shed our cares.
As the night wraps us in its embrace,
We dance with dreams in this sacred space.

Enigma of the Cosmic Canvas

A canvas vast, painted with stars,
We ponder the mysteries, near and far.
Each stroke a story, secrets entwined,
In the cosmos' poetry, we seek, we find.

Nebulas bloom in hues of gold,
Tales of the ancients silently told.
In the depths of space, time bends and flows,
A tapestry woven where wonder grows.

Galactic whirlpools spin and play,
Echoes of birth in celestial sway.
In patterns of light, chaos brings grace,
An enigma enveloped in infinite space.

We stand in awe, mere travelers lost,
In the dance of the cosmos, we count the cost.
Yet, in this puzzle, we find our place,
In the heart of the universe, a warm embrace.

Cosmic Waltz of the Heart

In the dance of the stars so bright,
Whispers of love take flight.
Galaxies spin in the velvet sky,
Two souls intertwined, never shy.

Orbits collide, a radiant glow,
Celestial bodies in a gentle flow.
Hearts beat to the cosmic tune,
In the night, love's sweet monsoon.

Time sways to the rhythm they make,
Through nebulas, their path they take.
Boundless dreams, horizons wide,
In this waltz, forever they glide.

Under starlit skies, they learn,
In their hearts, the universe turns.
A cosmic bond, never to part,
Eternal dance, the cosmic heart.

Enchanted by Nightfall

As the sun dips below the earth,
Whispers of dusk sing of rebirth.
Stars awaken, twinkling bright,
Inviting dreams in the coming night.

Moonlit paths, shadows play,
Magic stirs as the night gives way.
Gentle breezes sigh soft tunes,
Embraced by the glow of silver moons.

In this realm where magic brews,
Hearts entwined as hope renews.
In shadows deep, a story unfolds,
Night whispers secrets, brave and bold.

Lost in the magic, time stands still,
In the night's embrace, hearts can fill.
Enchanted souls in moonlit streams,
Awake the world with their dreams.

Twilight's Gentle Caress

When day surrenders to twilight's grace,
Soft hues linger, a warm embrace.
Golden and lavender, skies ignite,
In this fleeting, dreamy light.

Mountains whisper to oceans below,
As the night begins to flow.
Crickets chirp in a rhythmic tune,
While stars stretch out, ready to swoon.

In the silence, time whispers sweet,
The air is laced with love's heartbeat.
A gentle breeze wraps around the calm,
In twilight's arms, there lies a balm.

Moments freeze in the fading light,
Hearts align in the softest night.
With every breath, the world slows down,
In twilight's glow, love's crown.

Shadows of Stardust

In the quiet dusk, shadows dance,
Beneath the stars, they weave a trance.
Stardust whispers, secrets divine,
In the night's clasp, hearts align.

Glimmers of light in the deep, dark sea,
A cosmic embrace, wild and free.
Through endless skies, they drift and sway,
Guided by dreams that never fray.

As galaxies twirl in a grand parade,
Time drifts softly, unafraid.
With every heartbeat, new worlds await,
In shadows of stardust, they create.

Two souls adrift in an endless night,
Chasing the dawn, igniting the light.
Together they soar, forever entwined,
In shadows of stardust, love defined.

Whispers of the Midnight Sky

Stars twinkle like secrets untold,
In the silence, their stories unfold.
Moonlight drapes the world in silver,
A tranquil night, where dreams will quiver.

Breezes carry the night's sweet song,
Echoing where the shadows belong.
Whispers dance in the cool night air,
Inviting souls to linger and share.

In the stillness, wonders ignite,
The heart finds peace in the dark of night.
A canvas painted with cosmic grace,
Where time slows down, in this sacred space.

Under the stars, we find our way,
Guided by dreams that softly sway.
In the whispers of the midnight sky,
Our hearts take flight, as we learn to fly.

Celestial Reveries

In twilight's glow, the heavens gleam,
Wrapped in the warmth of a distant dream.
Nebulas whisper in colors so bright,
Painting the canvas of endless night.

Comets blaze with tales of the past,
A fleeting glimpse that fades too fast.
Each star a beacon of hope to behold,
A shimmering story, waiting to be told.

Constellations weave a tapestry grand,
Guiding lost travelers through cosmic land.
In celestial reveries, hearts take flight,
Drifting like stardust in the deep night.

Oh, to dance 'neath the cosmic affair,
Finding solace in the dark, still air.
In every sparkle, a promise we see,
A reminder of how vast dreams can be.

Nightfall's Embrace

As day surrenders to night's gentle grip,
Stars awaken, ready for their trip.
The moon sighs softly, casting her glow,
Wrapping the world in a tender show.

Whispers of shadows drift and sway,
In the depths of night, where secrets lay.
The dark unfolds stories lost in time,
Awakening hearts to a silent rhyme.

Nightfall's embrace, a comforting friend,
Invites the weary to find their blend.
In the silence, dreams begin to soar,
Each moment cherished, forevermore.

With every star that twinkles above,
We find our peace, feel the warmth of love.
In night's embrace, there's beauty to seek,
Where the soul finds strength and the heart can speak.

The Galaxy's Serenade

In the cosmos, melodies softly play,
Harmonies echo through the Milky Way.
Galaxies swirl in a cosmic dance,
Every note a spark, a chance romance.

Planets hum in deep, luscious tones,
Breathing life into the celestial zones.
With each twinkle, a story unfolds,
Of lovers and legends, of heroes bold.

The galaxy sings a lullaby sweet,
Guiding the weary, where dreamers meet.
In starlit realms, our spirits align,
In the serenade where stars brightly shine.

As night deepens, the symphony grows,
A cosmic embrace that endlessly glows.
In this vastness, we find our place,
The galaxy's serenade, a warm embrace.

Navigating the Night Universe

Stars whisper secrets, glowing bright,
In the dark canvas, dreams take flight.
Galaxies swirl, in a cosmic dance,
Charting the heavens, we take a chance.

Moonbeams guide our wandering way,
Casting shadows where nightbirds play.
Constellations map our fleeting thoughts,
In this celestial web, hope is sought.

Nebulae shimmer like jewels in space,
A vast ocean, each wave holds grace.
Sailing through silence, we find our peace,
In the vastness of night, our worries cease.

Among the stars, we find our song,
In the night universe, we all belong.
Navigating dreams, hand in hand,
Together we'll wander, across this land.

Beneath the Cosmic Veil

Wrapped in shadows, we softly sigh,
Under the vast, embracing sky.
Whispers of starlight dance on our skin,
Beneath the veil, new worlds begin.

Morning wishes wash over the land,
While night keeps secrets, quiet and grand.
In the cool air, the universe breathes,
With every rustle, a tale it weaves.

Mysteries linger in the midnight air,
Looming closer, we feel the dare.
For in that stillness, magic is born,
As we explore the night, never forlorn.

Beneath the cosmic veil, we dream,
Together as one, a radiant beam.
Holding hands through the galaxies wide,
In this sacred space, forever we glide.

Lunar Lullabies

The moon hums softly, a soothing tune,
Cradling the night in a silver swoon.
Stars blink in rhythm, joining the song,
Lullabies echo, where dreams belong.

Drifting on shadows, hearts intertwine,
As we chase starlight, through pathways divine.
In the cool glow, worries fade away,
Wrapped in the night, where children play.

Each twinkle a promise, each sigh a dream,
Moonlit wishes flow like a gentle stream.
In the soft stillness, love finds its way,
Singing sweet lullabies, come what may.

Under the watch of the celestial dome,
In lunar embraces, we find our home.
Together we'll wander, where shadows lie,
Listening closely to lunar lullabies.

A Tapestry of Nightlight

Threads of twilight, woven with care,
In the fabric of night, we find our share.
A tapestry bright, stitched by the stars,
Guiding our journey, near and far.

Each shimmer a story, each glow a word,
In this woven dreamscape, silence heard.
With gentle hands, the heavens create,
A masterpiece of love, never too late.

Sewn with hope, adorned with grace,
In every shadow, we find our place.
The night unveils wonders, vast and bright,
A gentle embrace in the warm moonlight.

So let us wander through this night art,
A tapestry of light, woven in heart.
Under the stars, our spirits soar high,
In this dance of darkness, we learn to fly.

Milton Keynes UK
Ingram Content Group UK Ltd.
UKHW021629011224
451755UK00010B/527

9 789916 906156